ONE
LIGHT

ONE LIGHT

A Poetry of Life, Dreams & Visions

John Lawrence Farmer

iUniverse, Inc.
New York   Bloomington

One Light
A Poetry of Life, Dreams & Visions

iUniverse books may be ordered through booksellers or by contacting:

iUniverse
1663 Liberty Drive
Bloomington, IN 47403
www.iuniverse.com
1-800-Authors (1-800-288-4677)

ISBN: 978-1-4401-1393-2 (pbk)
ISBN: 978-1-4401-1392-5 (ebk)

"The majority of the poems included in this compilation were previously registered with the Library of Congress, January 2003, under the title of One Light."

The artwork for the cover of One Light was created by Sandy Pond

Printed in the United States of America

iUniverse rev. date: 1/9/2009

To my Darling, Elizabeth, and our sweet Felisa

CONTENTS

INTRODUCTION

One Light is a compilation of poems that I wrote over a span of four years. This period was one of the most difficult of my life. Everything that I thought I was, or thought I possessed, was stripped away from me. Most of this occurred as fallout from my traumatic brain injury. The struggle to understand these events occupied my mind unceasingly. I questioned every aspect of life, love, and self-existence.

During this long process of soul-searching and contemplation, I started to have phrases that came to me, rising unexpectedly from my subconscious mind. These phrases and lines of prose were bits of answers that came to me in response to my quandary. The inspirations came at any time and place, so I began to write down the words immediately, on paper napkins, receipts, or whatever was at hand.

After a while, acquaintances and friends became curious about what I had been writing. I really had not planned to show my poems to anyone; I felt they were my personal outlet for all the angst and emotions I was feeling. Finally, I shared a few with the people I felt closest to, and was surprised by the

enthusiastic approval given. Gradually, I shared my poems with more and more people over the next few years, and was encouraged by a great many to publish them.

What I have been told repeatedly, is that my poems speak to the individuals that have read them. They find my manner of addressing the shared questions of life to be direct and simple, yet insightful. I am honored that so many have encouraged me to share my writing with a wider audience. The inspirations and realizations that I put forth are honest and true… to my mind, heart, and spirit. It is my sincere hope that those who read this book will find within it some thoughts that have real meaning in their lives… the contentment of the sense of resonance with Life itself.

John Lawrence Farmer
November 2008

One Light

The light we see/seek
In another's eyes,
We already know.
Why do we seek
To hold it apart…
A separate case?
For security, certainty, reassurance?
That Light is our Source,
Our Essence.
We know this is true
When we pass someone
We have never seen before…
Nor will we see again.
Yet we smile so,
To set one another alight—
That moment is truth, life.
In a way,
There is no greater meaning
To life itself.
Share the Light…
Share life.

Now

For good times passed
I laugh,
For good times passed
I cry.
It is not that I cling
To the past…
I live in the eternal Now,
Now living—now loving.
However…
Those moments seemingly gone,
Still live in their time—
The eternal Now
Past,
Even as moments in
The eternal Now
Future,
Have their part
In the whole.
Live each moment now
The best you can
With love as your guide…
Love eternal
Here, Now.

Expectation

So I ask
How can I improve?
The me
You want to see?
And you tell me
In all honesty!

So I accept
Thinking of all
I will gain.
After I have proven
Equal to the challenge...
My selfish expectations
Are not met—
You are not
The you
I wanted you to be!

Then I remember...
I change for my self
To be free.

Hopeful

Is hope
An expectation?
Separate souls come together
In agreement…
A hope of friendship
Bereft of anticipation,
No account kept…
Happiness & joy
Freely given,
No demands…
Vision clear.
Hope of sharing
Is no expectation!

Shadow of Doubt

When we met,
Did you perceive
A shadow of your fear?
Something hidden, buried inside?
Shadows shift,
Never the same—
Even though you thought
Similar.

Remember,
Only light *offset*
Yields a shadow…
Light in resonance
Yields no shadow.

Your Smile

Hope you don't mind
I fell into your smile…
It was so warm and open—
Invited me in
To stay for a while
And smile
In return.
A shared warmth…
Spiritual joy
Flowing through
Body and mind,
Wound around us
Resonating as one…
Until I couldn't tell,
Was it you or me?
Waking from that
Pleasant dream,
We were smiling still!

Lover

Who or what is a lover?
One who seeks to please
On all levels...
Pleasure given,
Only if they also take?
A lover—
One who loves
For the reward?
Imagine giving the
Kindness and attention
Of a lover,
Needing no reward
Except the pleasure
Of having given.

Selfless Perfection

The perfect love
Has many layers,
Levels of perception.
Should it be the
Holy mating pair...
Instinct of procreation?
Should it be
Selfish need,
Voraciously fulfilled
By everyone at once—
Despite all else?
Or should it be
Simple love of one another,
All selfless and free?

Trust Worthy

After we spend
All of our trust,
On someone
Who doesn't deserve it,
We feel foolish…
And swear never
To waste our trust again.
Slowly, we save it up
Month after month—
When brave enough,
Start sizing up others
Once more.
We reject one after another,
Finding small faults
Or inconsistencies
In very good people.
Until finally,
The pressure of this trust
And love saved up,
Strains at the gate—
And we find
We give it up,
Once again…
To a moment undeserving.
What is deserving?
When your trust,
Love, and passion
Meet their balance
In the other.
Remember… a balance
Requires both—
One alone,
Can not achieve it.

Message

The breezes play about my head,
My hair swirling to their rhythm.
Sounds of the promise of Life
Are borne to my ears…
I am never alone.
The winds can be terrible,
Crushing out our lives.
Yet they bring the rain
To sustain us.
These gusty messengers are
As the Spirit—
You never see them,
But their presence is always felt.

Agape

The love
That truly exists,
Can not be
Diminished or increased.
It is *the* love,
The constant of life…
Expressed as One
In all,
Animate and inanimate.
One love—
Simultaneously expressed,
In and out
Of time.

New Growth

Strange thing—
Even though you have gone
With another,
I feel you still…
Alive in my thoughts.
They say I should forget you…
After the resonance
We have known?

It takes dissonance
To mask the concert
Of kindred souls…
Dissonance to love?
Better to keep
The memory in warmth.
Life shall grow,
To include past glow
Without sorrow…
Life shall grow.

Modern Love

The next last time
We say goodbye…
I'm sure I will
Break down and cry.

The next last time
That we dance…
I'm sure I will
Jump at the chance.

The next last time
We make love…
I'm sure neither
Will get enough.

The next last time
Will keep on coming,
Despite our intent—
Coming, going, coming…

Freedom?

Alone
I sit on the wire,
A bird set free
From its cage.
Holding my breath,
Afraid of what may be…
Or not.
Swaying in the breezes
Of expectation and denial.
Have no fear
Of who I am…
I have no fear of you.
Different as opposite poles
We may be—
Just set one another free.

Definition

And so…
When you meet total emptiness,
Embrace it!
No more perfect definition—
Of who you are
As a separate perception
Within the whole,
The One—
Can be found,
Than in that moment.

Lost & Found

Pardon me…
But have you seen
My life?
I left it here
Amidst strife,
Passion
For self-
Satisfaction.
Realization—
You,
Me…
We should be
Harmony.

Self Aware

Sitting—
Watching my shadow
Mimic my actions,
I realized with a start…
To be too much aware
Of your self
Is like watching your shadow.
In harmony
With our Source,
The One Light…
We see no shadow.

Bookends

On this shelf
Of time/space…
You placed
Bookends for me.

A place to start…
We had an end.
The space between
Was worthy.

So it is…
I can still feel
As though
Between your bookends.

This shelf
Has no dust…
Always bright,
Never dimmed.

Thank you
My friend,
For my space
Upon your shelf.

Phoenix

I finally decided
To give it up…
A clever device!
"I will give it all away"
Till none is left—
My self gone,
Dissipated into all.
Then lo!
I grew instead.
In a rage,
For being denied
Self depletion…
I gave my last breath—
To find it was my first.

Dichotomy

I stand between
Two tempests—
My mind has fled
In fear.
The body longing for
Already felt pleasure…
The spirit knowing the joy
Of pure synergy.
Should the mind rejoin,
Let it be
Bereft of selfish want—
To understand that
All we have
Is being
One,
Together.

Clearly

Is it by the perfect Light
That I should see
Clearly—
Despite what I want to see?

For me to see
Simply
What is our synergy…
Harmony.
Then bathe me in that Light,
To ignite
My flight—
From the tyranny of me.

A Void

So I wanted
To have more.
The hole filled in,
Smoothed over…
My emotional voids
Bridged
By your soul…
Lost
To save mine…
Cost
Two souls…
In the One,
Redeemed.

Awareness

Life insists on
Experiencing *itself*,
Thus—
Our individual threads
In the weave of life,
The chorus of all…
What some thought
Music of the spheres…
Is the harmony
Of spirits,
Unified as one.

Hear

Give praise,
Even if it
Cannot be heard
By any one…
For the Universe
Will feel it
For all…
Resonance.

The Portal

I knocked
On heaven's door…
Begged a peek
Within—left without,
No crack revealed.

Again I rapped,
More vigor, more need…
"Open to me!"
I shouted—
Only silence met as I bled.

Both fists slammed
Against this gate,
Flailing, as I grew irate,
Passion roared…
Danced on hate.

How can I be denied?
I gave my life
To this tide
Of despair…
Again, I cried!

At last I turned,
Slumped away…
Leaving the entrance
To what could be—
And wasn't—opened to me.

One day I will return
Without my self.
That "time"
Shall know me,
And open wide.

Focus

There are no secrets…
Only keys
To understanding,
When the "lens"
Of the ego
Is clear.
No mysteries, either—
Only that which is
Not yet understood.

Celebration

You know the
"Secret",
When you realize
It doesn't matter…
Yet, the only thing
You can do,
Is to celebrate
And enable
One another…
Without concern
For self.
Then—
We live love!

Resonance

You say you are my friend...
In your eyes,
I see it is true.
The window to soul,
That shines
With the Essence
All share...
Resonant,
Complete.
My soul replies,
I am
The same to you...
No line between.
All that matters,
Is the degree
To which we agree...
The resonance
Of you and me.

The Dance

Drifting through
Space/time,
Tracing our paths
Around the Source,
Life's sun…
Separate bodies
Unconsciously finding
Attraction,
Repeatedly dancing—
The vortex of opposites
Sucks us in,
And spits us out
When unbalanced.

Gravity can make us
Crash and burn,
When we lose
Energy of stimulation.
If too alike,
We fear repulsion…
Complacency.
In truth,
When the dance of similar
Balances gravity…
True harmony—
The energy is infinite, perpetual.

Tracks

Pardon my
Feet of clay…
If they trod
Across your carpet,
And left their mark.
I can shed my shoes…
But not my humanity.

Shallow

How does it feel,
My empty love?
To be so in step
With this age?

The perfect fit—
You anointed us so.
Yet, as spoken,
You turned to go.

Hide your spirit,
Bury your soul…
If you dared
To feel it,
You could never
Let it go.

New View

Don't know—
Feeling blue.
Might go out…
How about you?

Been this way
For a while…
Think I remember
How to smile…

Seems I smile
At what is gone
Or not yet here—
The Present wrong?

In this view,
It is my sense
That is askew…
Unseen present tense.

If I can learn to smile
At what is here,
It can be perpetual…
Never a fear.

Actions

How many times
Louder
Do actions speak,
Than words?
Supposedly…
The more brazen the deed,
The less the explanation
Can soothe—
Thus, the kinder the action…
The truer the words?
The more convincing?
And how does this
Apply to self?
The degree of self-persuasion?
Hard to witness
One's own actions,
Making the self-talk
All the more convincing.
Perhaps we should
Carry a mirror with us,
To witness our selves…
To know what we are
Really doing.

Resistance

Is the cool pool
Of logic,
Derived from experience...
Immune, impervious to,
The heat of the moment?
Kept from boiling over?
How strong the wall,
Built with blocks of resolve—
To withstand tides of passion?
Kept from crumbling?
Shall it always be,
That the release is gained
By the antithesis?
The self-denied
Feared force,
Finally surrendered to?
Better to give
Each other
Peace of heart and mind...
By the synthesis
Of love, trust, and passion...
In harmony—
Joy and acceptance
Of who we can be,
In certainty.

Judgment

Now I know why
My feet are hot—

It is from the heat,
Contributed by those
Who apparently believe…
They have walked
In my shoes.
Psychic toe toast—
Best check their soles!

Ego Blind

"Saith man"—
From another's eyes,
I do not see…
Blind to all,
Except for me…
Ego mockery.

I can not be
As he…
To tell a life
How to be—
Only what it means
To be me…
Seeing what can be.

Soul Shine

Those shining eyes,
Whose light
Could ne'er be replaced…
Silhouette of soul
Expressed in her face…
A light,
Both felt and seen.
Mesmerized,
I thought by eyes…
Even though I saw
With more,
Than mine alone!

Athena

To Pallas Athena…
The spirit of all,
Distilled into flesh.
Cold?—Nay!
The perfect light,
And fire—
The essence of woman,
In perfect balance
With man—
Perfect passion!

Share

How sweet
Can life be?
The shared synergy
Of mind, soul, body...
You and me—
The harmony of We.

Complete

As one part
Of the totality,
Of the whole—
The answers
To every thought
Must exist...
Balanced
With all questions
That could be asked.

Know

I need to remember
It...
To remind others—
For, if I forget...
Who will remind me?

Symbiosis

Thank you insincerity,
For tempering my steel…
A depth of being,
You can not feel.

This gift of self,
Without the "ish"—
Is one unexpected,
You would not give.

You gave it the same,
Unconscious, unfeeling…
More than I would ask,
You gave me healing.

Your shallowness
Gave me depth…
Rejoice alone,
I hope you're next.

Present

If someone could tell,
When and why we meet
One another—
The air would be
Let out of the balloon.
The intricacy of discovery
O'er illumined…
To complacency.
The fire would pale.
And so it goes—
It eludes all,
Save the feel of
The Now.

Harmony

The resonant soul,
The resonant spirit…
Would you always know it,
If you came near it?

Or could you just go by,
Oblivious of the grace…
Lost in the distractions
Of time/space?

A heart of gold?
A pearl of great price?
None so precious,
As the resonant spirit.

Sensuous

Could the perfect azure sky,
Serene, yet electric…
Be found as a sweet light
In one's eyes?
It has in yours.

Could the silky touch
Of an unblemished rose,
Moist with a sweet dew…
Exist as a touch of one's lips?
It has in yours.

Could the gentlest caress
Of an evening zephyr,
Lightly dancing over skin and hair…
Be expressed by one's hand?
It has in yours.

If ever ones embrace
Could give perfect completeness,
Physical and spiritual…
Wholeness in the joining,
As yin-yang…
I found it in yours.

Untouched

I can feel your energy,
The quiver in your heart…
As my trembling hands
Stop themselves
From touching your face.
The touch I hesitate to give…
The touch you fear to receive…
Though we may desire it.
An inverse perfection,
An uneasy seesaw…
Seeking a balance
Of passion,
That the mind
Has not embraced—
Through touch—
Despite being wrapped
In the concept,
At times.
I can not touch,
For fear of uncertainty.
You can not be touched,
For fear of uncertainty.
Can any one know
How to heal the other,
Better than we?
For neither would touch
The other,
Unless it was true…
With trust and respect
Mutually.

Eye Light

If it is by reflected light,
This life we see…
And there is a light,
From the eyes of you and me…
Then truly, where the light
Of our eyes meet,
Is all we know—
Like the timeless pause
Lovers feel,
When totally immersed
In that sublime moment…
Seeing all eternity in each other.
Or in the first moment
You look into the open eyes
Of a newborn…
All eternity is there, too.
Each precious moment
You cannot name,
Is the shared dance
Of the light,
From the eyes of you and me.

One Heart

So, each time the heart is broken…
Is it as big when mended?
Or does it shrink, each time restored?
When you are able to give it again…
Is it a smaller thing to offer?
Or is it your will to give, that has shrunk?

Perhaps time alone can heal, somewhat—
A gap of time between, to lessen the emptiness felt.
New events and distractions to build a wall.
Is the wall made of insincerity, insensitivity, indifference?
Is the wall only behind to shield us from the past—
Or does it extend all around us,
Deflecting love as we go?

Rather, it is love that heals.
With the strength and care of true spirit…
The heart should heal complete.
For love comes from within and without.

That from within, comes from
The one love we all share.
That from without, comes from
All who share the love unconditionally.

And the beauty of a heart
Thus healed by one love,
Is that it has grown so large…
It cannot be broken.

Unconditional

Lost, in the profusion
Of love…
Surrounded, by so many
Worthy of love…
All.
I want to embrace
Our unity…
Celebration of life as one.

Yet instinct cries—
Take care of your own—
In ears and mind,
Telling us to exclude and abandon
Others…
For the sake of
Our self-persistence.

The one love, unconditional—
Eternity's being—is/was/will be,
Manifested by
The never separated spirit,
In our intertwined threads…
Outside time/space.

Refrain

Deliberate wallflower,
I became as stone…
Once upon the floor,
Now alone.

The music has left,
My soul withdrawn…
No passion to stir,
The dance unknown.

"Till I die"—
So I thought…
Self-imposed exile,
Endless drought.

Yet, as I dwelt
On sidelines…
Phantom-like,
Unperceived—

Ever beaconed the dance,
Never totally unseen…
Life's rhythm… music,
Never totally unheard.

'Till one day,
My soul opened again—
Embraced the dance,
Sang the song…

I will dance,
Long as I breathe…
Never again exiled,
Self-deceived.

Passion

Oscillatory,
The random light danced
In—
From her eyes.
The smile following…
Unfolding synchronistically,
With the rhythm
Of these flickers.
Staccato breathing
A harmonic,
To the pulsing tides
Of her heartbeat.
A slight shiver
Of eyelids,
To shutter briefly—
Never containing,
Nor constraining—
The passion light
That cascaded from her eyes,
Illuminating her face
With serenity.

Comfort

Even though we understand
The truth of selfless love,
Freely flowing to
One another...
Our sweet synergy
Emulating the One...
It is that self-aware
Need of comfort,
That inspires us.

Should we not
Recognize that,
Gladly give up
Selfish motivations,
And feed them
To the spirit fire?

Thus, we can glow
In the simple pleasure
Of sharing that comfort...
Giving to one another.

Persistence

Is the capacity
To feel love…
Another instinctual link?
Part of the drive to survive?
To keep in existence
Because of feeling loved,
Complete?
The more we feel love,
Taken and given…
The more we want to stay?

Perspective

If…
We could sit along side
Each other's thoughts,
Just briefly…
As a guest, a visitor…
Understand what each other
Was… Is,
Maybe we would have
No fear,
Prejudice,
Hate,
War…
One love.

Sweetness

Take it for the sweetness...
Never think it is yours alone.
If you need to know
How hard it is to give...
Just look inside yourself.

We have not a thing,
Except that which is freely given.
When it comes,
Bless it... nourish it,
Then release it.
Give it back—
Pass it on when you can.

This feeling so sweet,
Makes us want to keep it
For ourselves—
Yet it is sweet,
Only in the sharing...
Else it could not exist.
So take it for the sweetness,
And give it when you can.

Soul Mating

To what...
Am I making love?
Your face—your beauty?
Your heart—your body?
Your self—your being?

If only I could feel
Your soul inside me...
Same time mine
Is inside you...
Every time.

All rhythms
Within us
Merged...
No more me
Or you...
Making love
To life itself...
As one.

Reunited

Should self-love
Be achieved
By lofty removal
Of self—
From all else?

Or is it gained
By the selfless giving,
Of one
To another—?
Until alight
From the unified fire
As one… here, Now—
All selves loved by all.

Nectar

Sweet sisters,
Sweet brothers…
You are so
Because—
You taste and drink deeply
Of the sweet Essence
Of life…
Then give it back,
Without it souring
In the intensity
Of indifference, or selfishness encountered.
Let us be the vessels
To pour the sweet Essence
Into one another—
Each filling the other completely…
No one ever empty.

Self-Contained

I am not immortal…
I cannot be the One.
The whole universe
Won't fit inside me.
Cram infinity,
Into a five-pound bag?
However, I share
The same Essence,
With the whole universe.
In that sharing,
We are as one…
Forget the bag!

Unbounded

So I give…
You receive.
You give…
I receive.

What are the boundaries,
Of what we perceive
To be "right" or "enough"…
A balance?

What could not
Be given?

The Song

Some are the dancers…
Some are the song.
When I sing,
I do not need
To dance.
When they dance,
They do not need
To sing.

Sometimes,
I dance
As I sing—
Sometimes,
They sing
As they dance—
Interwoven,
We complete the song…
The music.

Rejoice and manifest
The beauty of life,
Do your part…
While holding
The other,
In your heart.

Ironic

Irony…
Iron me
Flat as a sheet—
Blank canvas
Undefined—
Re-invent me.

Time and again,
Thought it made sense—
Seemed like the trigger
For your intents—
Kaleidoscope turn…
New universe sent.

Perception is weak
Against your tide—
Nothing certain,
All untied…
Unraveled as
The moment described.

Yet through these shifts,
I have known beauty.
The colored bits of glory,
Numbered, in your case—
The new display,
New life discovered.

Sweet irony,
Always new—
Eternal chaos,
Somehow seen through…
I am re-assembled
Through your view!

Reflection

Why should reflection
Exist...?
For self-awareness?
For self-examination?
For self-knowledge?

So, do we reflect upon...
The light shown?
The image seen?
The mind known?

There is only one reason,
For this looking glass...
To remember what
We are,
Have been,
Will be...

Let us reflect.

One Breath

The sweetest breath tasted,
Is the one shared with your lover…
The one you cannot tell
If drawn or released—
Pausing on the threshold as one
The perfection of shared breath…
Shared light flashing through the eyes
Feeling yourself through the other's touch
All freely given to the other
A beauty and ecstasy created together
A moment timeless in united joy.

Feel

O Great creator!

How can it be…?
That eternal spirits
Of fire
Should burn in flesh
So paper thin!

Sensation

Epitome of
Physical love…
Is like the
Simultaneous explosion
Of
Two supernovae,
In intimate proximity!

True Love

And so we pretend…
That the greatest thing
We can give,
Is our physical love—
The progenitor of genetic continuance,
The basic instinctive response,
Driven by survival…
This is the wheel of karma!

We grow and truly love,
When this illusion is dispelled by
The simultaneously expressed giving of
Our whole selves—the universal love—
In a united understanding
That all we are,
Is our one love
Freely given…
With no division.

Day Dreams

Every time
I go to sleep,
I wonder if
I'll fall too deep...

To reappear
Where I left,
An individual
Somewhat obsessed...

Confused by this
Single mind—
When awake, pondering
The dreams left behind.

One-Another

The strength you have,
You expect in others.
But we all have
Different strengths…
One from the other.
To recognize
Another's strength
Is to become stronger.

When all acknowledge
One another's strength
Simultaneously,
We shall be as one…
Here, Now.

Fruition

I know humanity
Carries the seed
Of love and giving
Within itself—
To worry about
The self
Is just instinct—
Individual continuance…
Illusion of immortality.

To all nurture love
Together…
Is our synergy of spirit,
As one.

The Singer

You hear that voice,
And you think
Perhaps
It is The Voice…
Because the singer's
Sweet resonance
Echoes the purity
Of the Source.
That voice
Is but one,
In the choir of The Voice…
One with what it speaks—
Mind, spirit, and body
In perfect harmony.

The Blessing

Bless you lord—
Say what?
That a "me"
Should utter such
A phrase…
To presume?
Yet, in truth…
So connected are we
In the One,
That a blessing spoken
By one
Is for all…
In unity.
The blessing of life,
Unto itself.

Homecoming

Did you ever long
For that place called home…
Tho' you might not know, where it may be?
Did you ever feel the warmth within,
And think that it was real?
Did the strength—of feeling complete—
Fill your heart to overflow?
A joy vibrating so powerfully and sweet,
No restraint could make it be withheld—

Then you have grazed against
The spirit of one,
The joy of life we share.
A fullness that cannot be told…
Only felt, within each soul.
To take this exuberant joy,
And radiate it back
To everyone…
Is the simplicity of truth.
We are all home,
When we are one.

Tapestry

I am as
A single thread,
Looking back…
The tapestry
Unraveling,
Nearly undone.

Our shared vision
Dissolving—
Vapor,
Before our eyes.

Just
As the last knot
Untied,
The weave began
To restore.

Till again
Pattern in place,
Tapestry redone…
Whole once more.

The image is new,
The names all changed—
The threads within,
Always the same.

The Circle

At age twenty eight, I was visited by an exceptionally lucid dream, unique in its energy and authenticity. It was in vibrant color, all my senses engaged and focused. As it unfolded, I was absolutely convinced it was true as it happened, moment by moment.

I become aware that I am walking down a long corridor, which stretches before me. It is filled with bright sunlight; warm and golden… yet silver and cool in its feel. As if, it is of the spirit… a complete light. As I walk calmly and deliberately, I can see the light is flooding in through very large windows on both sides of the corridor. The windows remind me of those in a church, with the tops arched into a point.

I am somewhat surprised that there is no stained glass upon recognizing that shape. In fact, there is nothing visible outside of the windows… the windows are all glowing uniformly with that splendid light. Also, I am aware of occasional doors

on each side, but I do not pause or examine them closely. The light seems to resonate with the amber tones of the wood from the floor before me, and with the wood of the doors, doorways, and window frames. It is as if this golden wood is from some ancient variety that glows from within.

As I proceed, I hear my footsteps on the floor, and the faint echoes from them. Somehow, I feel like I am radiating the energy of that place, even as I absorb it. At this point, it appears I am walking down a hall that extends forever, no end visible. It feels like I am in a grand, ageless mansion that is immense and endless in size.

Minute after minute I continue, passing doors, and windows without number. I do not know where I am headed, yet I feel that all is well, and have no doubts or hesitation. At last, I see the posts and banisters of a large, sweeping stairway on the left side of the corridor.

Everything is aglow in that spirit light. Then, as I come to the opening of the stairway, a brilliant white light, at the left side of the opening, strikes my eyes. As intense as it is, the light is not blinding.

This light is emanating from an immense chandelier, made entirely of perfect, flawless crystal. It is breath taking! I pause for the first time, to look for the ceiling, wanting to see how far the chandelier extends. However, it spirals up and up, tier after magnificent tier of concentric circles, beyond my limit of vision.

Pausing there, at the head of the stairs, I am mesmerized by the myriad of sparkles that shoot from this cascade of crystal. It is like the twinkle of

all the stars from all the galaxies dancing in my eyes. It is so beautiful, so perfect.

Then I turn my attention back to the stairway itself. It too is of that golden wood, and it is very wide. Splendid banisters flank both sides, and I see that it bends gracefully to the left as it descends. Furthermore, I can see that it empties out onto a vast floor made of that same ancient wood.

Without feeling prodded or directed, I become aware that I should descend the stairs in front of me. I start to walk down the wide staircase, looking to my left at the chandelier. It seems just barely out of reach, past the left banister.

As I progress downward, I can see that I am entering an immense room— again without perceivable limits! Like a vast ballroom, flooded with the same surreal light… but from windows on walls I cannot see. Still, all is at peace, and my whole being is aglow. It is so serene!

Looking out upon that room as I reach the final few steps, I can see other people. They are seated on the floor, a short distance ahead. Now, as I approach the group, I can see they are sitting in a huge circle. There are scores of people there, holding one another's hands.

Drawing closer and closer, I can see there is an opening in the circle. As I approach the opening, I am startled to realize that I recognize every face in that group! This is the first intense emotion I have felt. They are friends and family, some alive, and some who have passed on. Also, there are some who I do not remember from this lifetime, but I know and love them all as well. My feelings are happiness

and joy at seeing them, for they are all wonderfully alive, here and now!

Standing just outside of the opening in the circle, I see loving smiles from all faces. Bliss washes over me, and I seat myself into the opening, feeling my own broad smile from ear to ear. As I sit, cross-legged, I reach to the hands on each side of me, and hold them firmly, yet tenderly.

For a short while, I look around this vast circle and bask in the Love from all of these souls. Then, I look to my right, and see that a close friend named Sue is sitting there. She is a sweet person, sincere and friendly by nature.

Seeing her surprises me a little, and I just say "Hi Sue" She is smiling in a warm and caring way… yet I sense she has a trace of a secret in that smile. A secret that I already know, but need to acknowledge.

Suddenly, with shock, I realize this is a dream! To my extreme surprise, nothing changes. I am still alive and aware in all my senses in this dream, seeing her face barely two feet away from mine. Amazed, I lean in closer and study her eyes and face. It is Sue, no doubt!

Her smile broadens even more, and I can sense her physical self in its nearness, just as if I was awake. I can even see her eyes moving just slightly back and forth, as she focuses on my eyes, one, and then the other.

At this moment, a question comes to me, and I ask it even as it is forming. Still eye-to-eye, with me earnestly taking in every nuance, I ask, "Sue, I just realized… this is a dream, and you are with me in

it. Can you tell me if you are dreaming too, and am I in yours?"

Her eyes widen slightly, and her mouth starts to open to give the reply, and… Instantly, I am awake! Desperately, I close my eyes, and strain to see her face and hear her answer… to no avail.

The rest of the night was spent in wonder and excitement. I was so energized by the experience that I found it impossible to sleep. I could not wait to see Sue, to discover if she had that dream too! I half expected her to call that night, to tell me she had experienced the same dream.

When next I talked to Sue, I found she had not shared that dream, at least not to her recollection. I admit I was disappointed at first, but only because I had so much wanted this verification. Because of my excited anticipation, I mistakenly thought such an agreement was necessary for a clear and undeniable proof of the higher plane of the mind and spirit.

Upon further reflection, however, I realized that I had missed the real importance of what had been revealed. The dream was for me, not Sue or any one else, for that matter. We each have our own lessons, insights, and dreams. They come to us individually, when appropriate for our own lives and growth.

That vision has infused me with an essential confidence in the higher consciousness. An awakening of an intrinsic knowledge we already possess. It was a precious glimpse into what awaits us, beyond this life.

I rejoice in the sweet assurance of the Reunion to come!